This is a Let's-Read-and-Find-Out Science Book™

BITS and BYTES

A Computer Dictionary for Beginners

By SEYMOUR SIMON

Illustrated by Barbara and Ed Emberley

A Computer Book
3

Thomas Y. Crowell   New York

Other Recent Let's-Read-and-Find-Out Science Books™ You Will Enjoy

Sunshine Makes the Seasons · The BASIC Book · Hurricane Watch · My Visit to the Dinosaurs · Meet the Computer · Flash, Crash, Rumble, and Roll · Volcanoes · Dinosaurs Are Different · Germs Make Me Sick! · What Happens to a Hamburger · How to Talk to Your Computer · Comets · Rock Collecting · Is There Life in Outer Space? · All Kinds of Feet · Flying Giants of Long Ago · Rain and Hail · Why I Cough, Sneeze, Shiver, Hiccup, & Yawn · You Can't Make a Move Without Your Muscles · The Sky Is Full of Stars · The Planets in Our Solar System · Digging Up Dinosaurs · No Measles, No Mumps for Me · When Birds Change Their Feathers · Birds Are Flying · A Jellyfish Is Not a Fish · Cactus in the Desert · Me and My Family Tree · Redwoods Are the Tallest Trees in the World · Shells Are Skeletons · Caves · Wild and Woolly Mammoths · The March of the Lemmings · Corals · Energy from the Sun · Corn Is Maize · The Eel's Strange Journey

The *Let's-Read-and-Find-Out Science Book* series was originated by Dr. Franklyn M. Branley, Astronomer Emeritus and former Chairman of The American Museum–Hayden Planetarium, and was formerly co-edited by him and Dr. Roma Gans, Professor Emeritus of Childhood Education, Teachers College, Columbia University. For a complete catalog of Let's-Read-and-Find-Out Science Books, write to Thomas Y. Crowell Junior Books, 10 East 53rd Street, New York, NY 10022.

Bits and Bytes: A Computer Dictionary for Beginners
Text copyright © 1985 by Seymour Simon
Illustrations copyright © 1985 by Ed Emberley
Printed in the U.S.A. All rights reserved.
Designed by Al Cetta
1 2 3 4 5 6 7 8 9 10
First Edition

Library of Congress Cataloging in Publication Data
Simon, Seymour.
  Bits and bytes.

  (Let's-read-and-find-out science book)
  Summary: A dictionary of computer terms explaining parts, functions, and useful jargon.
  1. Computers—Dictionaries, Juvenile. 2. Electronic data processing—Dictionaries, Juvenile. [1. Computers—Dictionaries. 2. Data processing—Dictionaries]
I. Emberley, Barbara, ill. II. Emberley, Ed, ill.
III. Title. IV. Series.
QA76.15.S49 1985   001.64'03'21   85-47533
ISBN 0-690-04474-7
ISBN 0-690-04475-5 (lib. bdg.)

BITS and BYTES

How many bytes are in a computer's RAM?
What happens when you boot a computer?
Does your computer have a mouse?

These questions may sound silly, but they all use common computer words. Some of the words, such as bit and bug, are ones you know, but in computer talk they have different meanings. Other words, such as cursor and graphics, may be new to you.

This book will help you to use and understand the most commonly used computer words. Soon you'll be able to say, "My computer crashed, but I had a backup of the program and didn't lose any data"—and know what you mean!

WHEN YOU SEE A WORD IN CAPITAL LETTERS, LIKE THIS OR THIS, IT MEANS YOU CAN LOOK THAT WORD UP IN THIS BOOK, TOO!

Access—To get information or DATA from a computer's MEMORY.

Accessing information is like looking up something in a book. But it usually takes only a second or two to access information from a computer.

Address—A particular spot in a computer's MEMORY. Each address has its own number and can store one piece of information. The numbers help the computer quickly locate information in its memory.

Backup—A copy of a computer PROGRAM. Suppose you write a program and SAVE it on a DISK or CASSETTE. You might make a backup copy of the program in case you lose or damage the original. You usually copy a program onto another disk or cassette.

BASIC—A computer language. BASIC is used with many home computers. BASIC uses many English words, such as PRINT, END, and RUN. The word BASIC is short for <u>B</u>eginner's <u>A</u>ll-purpose <u>S</u>ymbolic <u>I</u>nstruction <u>C</u>ode.

Bit—The smallest piece of information or DATA that a computer can use. The word bit stands for <u>BI</u>nary digi<u>T</u>. Binary means two, so a bit can be either one of two digits, 0 or 1.

Boot—To start a computer. Most computers boot automatically when you switch on the power. When a computer boots, it takes operating instructions from ROM and puts them into its temporary MEMORY or RAM. Then the computer is ready for whatever you want it to do.

Break—To stop a PROGRAM while it is running. Many computers have a break key. When you press the key, the computer stops what it is doing. When you want to continue the program you have to RUN it again.

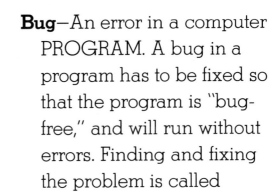

Bug—An error in a computer PROGRAM. A bug in a program has to be fixed so that the program is "bug-free," and will run without errors. Finding and fixing the problem is called "debugging."

Byte—One byte is eight BITS. Each byte stands for a letter, a symbol (such as a question mark), or a number. For example, the word "truck" needs five bytes. Can you tell how many bytes your name would need?

Cartridge—A plastic case with a ROM CHIP in it. A cartridge usually fits into an opening in the back or side of a home computer. The ROM chip in a cartridge might contain a game PROGRAM, for example, or a computer language program such as BASIC.

1101	0100	= T
1101	0010	= R
1101	0101	= U
1100	0011	= C
1100	1011	= K

CHIP →

SPACE MISSION

Cassette—A plastic case with a spool of recording tape in it. A cassette tape, like a CARTRIDGE, might contain a game or some other kind of computer PROGRAM. A cassette used with a computer is similar to a cassette used for music recording.

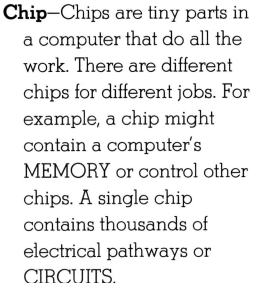

RECORDING TAPE

Chip—Chips are tiny parts in a computer that do all the work. There are different chips for different jobs. For example, a chip might contain a computer's MEMORY or control other chips. A single chip contains thousands of electrical pathways or CIRCUITS.

Circuit—An electrical pathway. There are many different kinds of circuits in a computer.

Computer—A machine that works with, or processes, information or DATA that you give it. The computer uses a PROGRAM that tells it what to do. All the information is stored in the computer's MEMORY. The computer uses a CPU, its "brain," to do arithmetic, play a game, draw a picture, or do many other things.

BEEP....
BEEP
BOOP

CPU—A CHIP that is the "brain" of the computer. It does the actual computing, or PROCESSING. It also controls all the other chips in the computer. CPU is short for <u>C</u>entral <u>P</u>rocessing <u>U</u>nit.

Crash—When the computer suddenly stops working.

CRT—The picture tube, or screen, in a television set or MONITOR. CRT stands for <u>C</u>athode <u>R</u>ay <u>T</u>ube.

Cursor—A blinking dot or short line on the screen. The cursor marks the place on the screen where the next letter or symbol you type will appear.

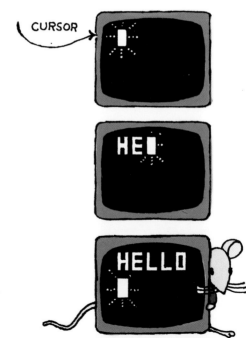

CURSOR

Data—Information that you INPUT to a computer, or that the computer OUTPUTS.

Disk—A round, flat, plastic "record" that is sealed in a square cardboard holder. The disk stays in the holder even while it is "played." The disk is used to store a PROGRAM or DATA. Because disks are thin and flexible, they are called "floppy disks" or "floppies."

Disk drive—A disk "player" that runs the disk. It can READ the information on the disk or WRITE new information on the disk.

Display—What you see on a CRT screen.

CLICK

WHIRR WHIRR

SPACE MISSION

File—A collection of related information or DATA. For example, a list of the batting averages of the players on a baseball team can be a file. Any computer PROGRAM can be a file, too.

GIGO—Stands for <u>G</u>arbage <u>In</u>, <u>G</u>arbage <u>O</u>ut. It means that if you put wrong information into the computer, wrong information will come out.

Graphics—Pictures on a CRT screen.

Hardware—The parts of a computer that you can touch, such as the KEYBOARD, the MONITOR, and the DISK DRIVE, as well as all the parts inside.

Input—DATA transferred to a computer from a DISK or CASSETTE, or put into the computer by using a KEYBOARD or JOYSTICK.

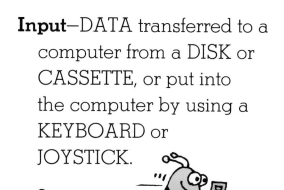

Also, to give data to a computer.

Joystick—A box with a lever on top. The joystick is attached to a PORT on the computer. When you move the lever in any direction it sends a signal to the computer. A joystick may be used to make the moves in a game or to draw pictures on the screen.

K—Short for <u>K</u>ilobyte, or about one thousand BYTES of MEMORY. For example, a 64K computer means it has about sixty-four thousand bytes of computer memory. An 8K RAM chip can store about eight thousand bytes.

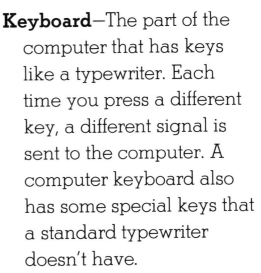

Keyboard—The part of the computer that has keys like a typewriter. Each time you press a different key, a different signal is sent to the computer. A computer keyboard also has some special keys that a standard typewriter doesn't have.

Load—To put a PROGRAM into a computer.

Logo—A computer language that is easy for beginners to learn. Logo lets you draw pictures on the screen with a "turtle."

"TURTLE"

LOGO PICTURES→

DISK DRIVE PROGRAM COMPUTER

Memory—The chips in a computer that store DATA and PROGRAMS. A computer has two different kinds of memory, RAM and ROM.

Microprocessor—A CHIP that controls the workings of the computer. Microprocessor is another name for the CPU. A microprocessor is sometimes called a "computer on a chip."

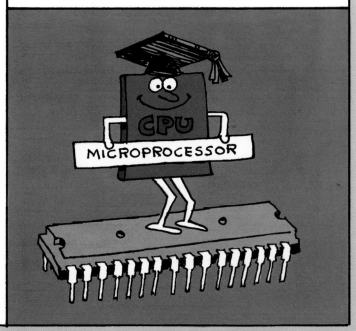

Monitor—A CRT connected to a computer. A monitor is like a television set, but it has no buttons or dials for selecting channels. Some TVs can be used as monitors, too.

Mouse—A small machine connected to a computer by a cable (its "tail"). When you roll the mouse around on a flat surface, you make the CURSOR move on the screen. A mouse also has a button or two that you can press to make the computer do different things.

CHANNEL SELECTORS

← TV

MONITOR ←

MOUSE

"TAIL"

Output—The DATA a computer sends out from its MEMORY. Output can be words or pictures. It can appear on a monitor or on a PRINTER. Also, to send out data to a monitor or a printer.

Peripheral—Any machine that is connected to a computer. A MONITOR, a DISK DRIVE, and a PRINTER are examples of peripherals.

Port—A place in a computer where a PRINTER, a MONITOR, or some other PERIPHERAL can be connected.

Printer—A machine that prints a computer's OUTPUT on paper.

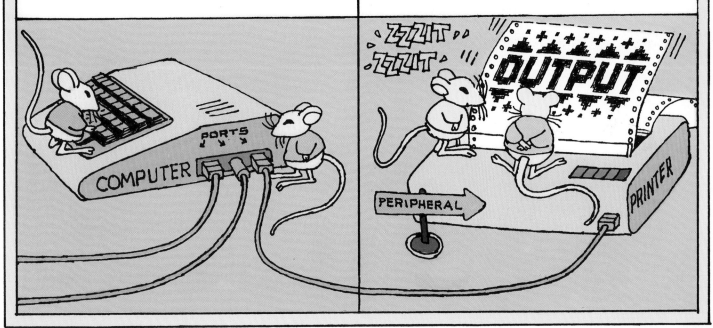

Processing–The actual work, or computing, done by a computer.

Program–A set of instructions for a computer to follow. Programs can be written in BASIC, in LOGO, or in some other computer language. People who write programs are called programmers.

RAM—A kind of temporary, or "scratch pad," MEMORY on a CHIP. You can store information in RAM for as long as it is needed. When you shut off power to the computer, all the information is lost from RAM. RAM stands for <u>R</u>andom <u>A</u>ccess <u>M</u>emory.

Read—To get information from the CASSETTE, CARTRIDGE, or DISK on which it has been stored. The information is put into the computer's RAM. Reading copies the information, but doesn't erase it from the storage place.

ROM—A MEMORY CHIP.
ROM contains instructions for the computer that were put in at the factory where the chip was made. The information stored in ROM remains there even when you turn off the power to the computer. ROM stands for <u>R</u>ead <u>O</u>nly <u>M</u>emory.

Run—To start using a PROGRAM.

Save—To store information from a computer's RAM on a CASSETTE or DISK. You save information so that it will not be lost when you turn off the computer. You have to WRITE the information to save it.

Software—The PROGRAMS used by a computer. CASSETTES, CARTRIDGES, and DISKS are also called software.

Word Processing—A way of using a computer as a kind of super typewriter. A word processing program lets you write, change the order of words or sentences, and make corrections. When all your changes are made, you can use a PRINTER to make a neat copy of what you have written.

Write—To put information from the computer's RAM on a CASSETTE or DISK. You write information so you can SAVE it.

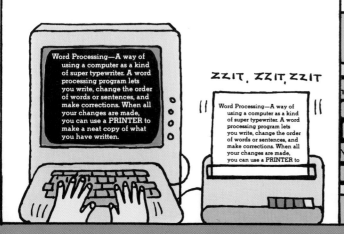

ZZIT, ZZIT, ZZIT

WHIRR WHIRR

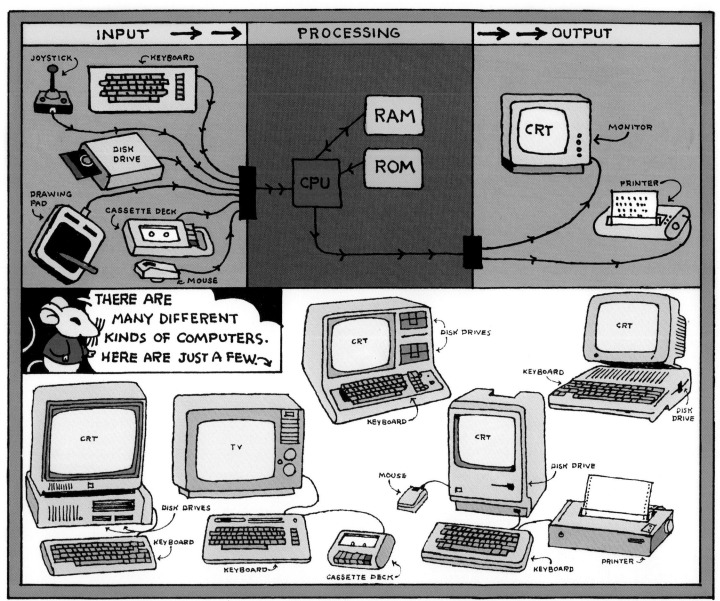

Seymour Simon was a science teacher for a number of years and now writes and edits full time. He is the author of dozens of highly acclaimed science books for young readers, including MEET THE COMPUTER; HOW TO TALK TO YOUR COMPUTER; THE BASIC BOOK; COMPUTER SENSE, COMPUTER NONSENSE; and THE DINOSAUR IS THE BIGGEST ANIMAL THAT EVER LIVED AND OTHER WRONG IDEAS YOU THOUGHT WERE TRUE. He has also written YOUR FIRST HOME COMPUTER, a book for adults. More than thirty of Mr. Simon's books for young readers have been selected as Outstanding Science Trade Books for Children by the National Science Teachers Association.

Ed Emberley has written and illustrated many popular children's books, including ED EMBERLEY'S DRAWING BOOK OF ANIMALS. He and his wife, **Barbara Emberley**, have collaborated on several books, most notably DRUMMER HOFF, winner of the 1968 Caldecott Medal.

Mr. and Mrs. Emberley have illustrated other Let's-Read-and-Find-Out Science Books, including MEET THE COMPUTER, HOW TO TALK TO YOUR COMPUTER, THE BASIC BOOK, and FLASH, CRASH, RUMBLE, AND ROLL.